CW00524396

DENIS WRIGLEY

The living world of the

SEASHORE

A Wrigley Eye Opener

LUTTERWORTH PRESS
Guildford and London

Here, where the sea breeze blows salt to our lips,
and the sounds of the sea fill our ears,
the land ends and the water begins…

What can live in this place
that's partly covered with salt water
for half the day?
How will it survive when the tide goes out,
here along the shore that's pounded by the force
of the waves, in cold temperatures and hot?

The waves crash on the beach, sometimes cold,
green and foaming, sometimes blue in the sunshine.
They bring flotsam and jetsam—pieces of wood,
things dropped from ships—and seaweed.
Each day the sea advances and retreats,
covering the beach with salt water
and leaving a line of refuse—
the HIGH TIDE LINE.

On this high water line shells and insects
and all sorts of creatures make their homes
amongst the living and dead waste.

Above the high water mark is the SPLASH ZONE.
Here above the waves but where the spray splashes
you may find lichens and winkles
and sandhoppers. There's something
new to look for in all parts of the beach.

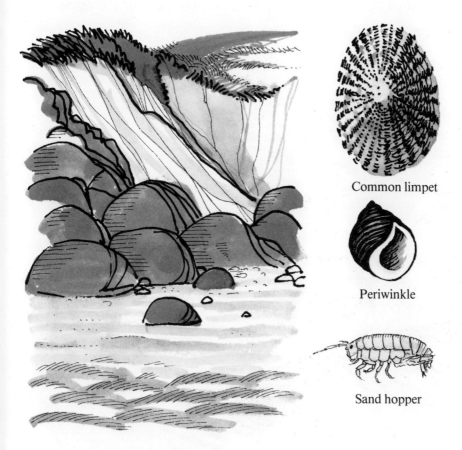

Common limpet

Periwinkle

Sand hopper

The wavelets leave their
mark on a sandy shore.
Look for these ripples.

Everything that lives depends on something else.
Plants make food for animals and these are food
for others. Little fish and shellfish eat tiny
microscopic plant life called plankton.
Big fish eat little fish and so on…
All of them have some means of attack or defence—
such as claws, pincers, beaks or teeth.

Some are protected by the colours and patterns
on their bodies and shells that make them
difficult to see. Some send out jets of
inky liquid
and crabs even lose their limbs easily to help them
escape when attacked!

Sea hare ejects a
purple dye
when alarmed.

The claw of
a crab has
a built-in
breaking point.
The crab loses a
claw to escape
and can grow another
one.

The boats lie drawn up above the high tide mark.
Below them lichens and seaweeds grow
marking the line where the high water reaches.

Barnacles—
closed and open

Shelled animals, like barnacles and winkles,
cling to the rocks below this line.
Protected by its shell the living barnacle
needs air and water to live. The moment the tide
leaves it dry its shell closes, trapping air
and water inside to allow the barnacle to live
till the sea returns. Under water the shells
open to let thin, bristly legs come out
to collect food.

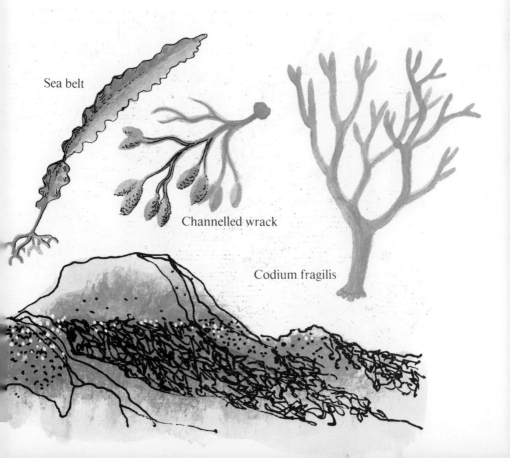

Sea belt

Channelled wrack

Codium fragilis

The tide goes out and leaves behind it
rock pools where water is trapped in hollows,
forming little worlds full of life:
fascinating places where you can look for
little crabs and star fish, sea anemones and
prawns.

In this part of the shore there are many kinds
of seaweed. They look flat and floppy
lying on the rocks, but they are the woods
and forests of the sea. In the movement of water
they wave to and fro while fish flit through
them like birds through trees.

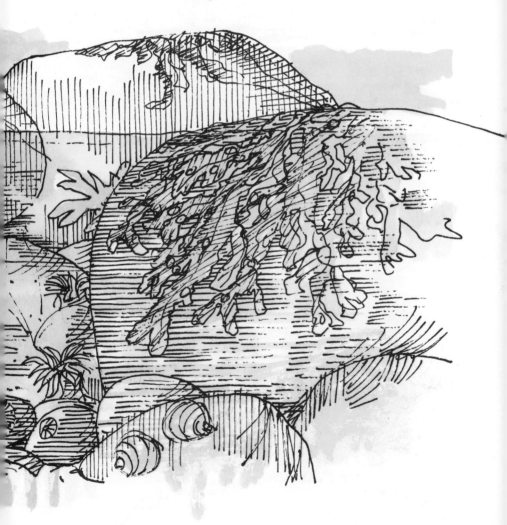

Beaches can be rocky or stony, muddy or sandy.
A beach may look flat and empty—a deserted
sea bed—but many living things lie on and
beneath its surface.

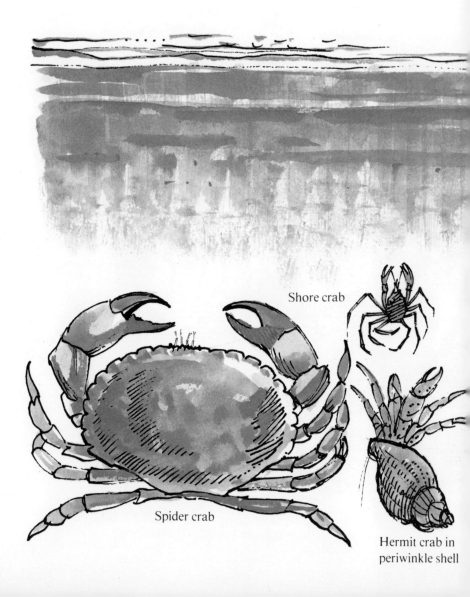

Shore crab

Spider crab

Hermit crab in
periwinkle shell

There are many kinds of worms, lug worms, for
instance. You may see little piles of sand
on the surface…worm casts. Worms, burrowed
beneath the sand, have swallowed and
extracted anything edible from the sand
and passed out these piles of waste.

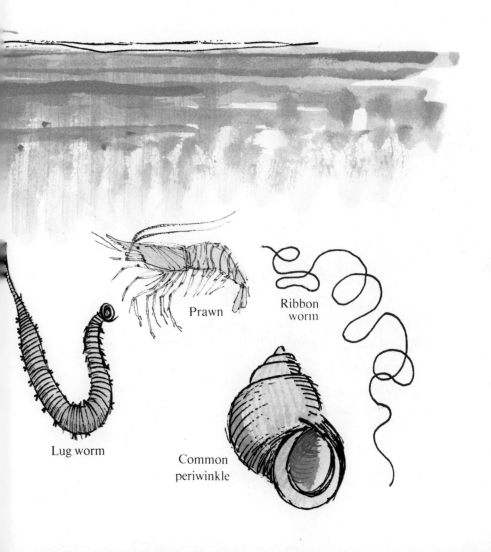

Prawn

Ribbon
worm

Lug worm

Common
periwinkle

Sea shores are not all the same. They may be
formed from different rocks or be in different
climates and so you may also find different
plants or animals on your beach from those
on another, but in each case there is the sea
changing the shape of the coast and
affecting the life in it and by it.

Scurvy
grass

The salt of the sea affects the plants of the
coast. Gusts of wind blow from the sea
to the land carrying salt and sand to smother
and kill plants.
The force of the air, as it moves between
land and sea, bends the trees before it.
Things survive that adapt to the conditions
they live in and trees would snap if they
didn't bend!

nged sea lavender

The land slopes upwards from the sea. The sea
shapes the coast, sometimes dropping silt and
stones carried in its waters, sometimes
with the cutting force of its driving waves.
In places the land has been cut into cliffs—
rugged and harsh, sometimes with plants
clinging to their rough surfaces. Here birds
build their nests in cracks and crevices,
on shelves and projecting rocks.
Listen to their cries, the sound of the waves,
and noise of the wind…the seashore can be
a noisy place and a wild one!

The changing coast. The sea deposits
gravel, sand or pebble to form new shores
and cuts away existing shores and cliffs.

Fish, refuse from passing ships, scraps
found along the seashore, snails,
even the eggs of other birds, all provide
food for seabirds. Watch them eating.
Some fly high, ready to dive swiftly on
fish seen clearly under the sea.

Look for the shapes of the sea birds'
beaks adapted to their method of
catching food.

Others strut beside the breaking waves, long
beaks ready to probe the mud or sand. Some are
solitary whilst others flock together. Look
for them, watch their
different habits.
The sea sometimes brings death to birds.
Oil from tankers and other ships can clog the feathers
and prevent birds from flying.

Common
gull

Fulmar

Avocet

Oyster catcher

Common tern

Above the waves the air is full of sound and
movement, but in the silent world
below the surface, life of a different kind
comes to the shore.
When covered with water the shore becomes
the bed of the sea. Look at the gleaming scales
of the fishes and the weeds moving
in the water currents. This is the underwater
picture to remember when the tide has gone out.

Wet, still, from the water of high tide
a sandy beach gleams in the sunshine.
Can you see where the feet of birds and
someone's toes have sunk in the damp sand,
leaving their tracks?
Each day the tides bring new food to the
creatures under the sand. As it covers the
beach the water carries fresh supplies
of brine and other food materials.
These are left behind as the tide recedes.

You won't find the fish of the deep waters here
but if you look through the clear, shallow
waters at low tide you may see shoals of little
fish—now you see them, then, swiftly
they've gone!
On the sand are shells of many shapes,
some occupied and some no longer lived in.
You may find sea urchins and other things
that live in the shallow water.

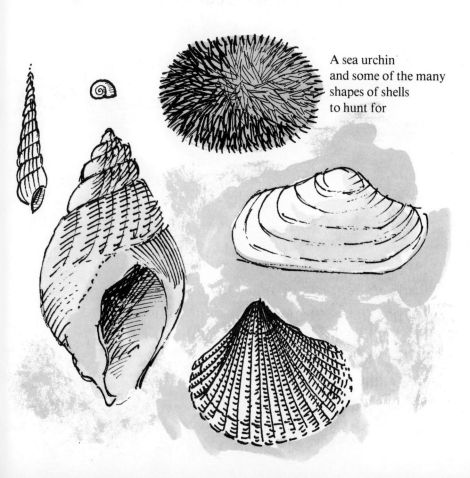

A sea urchin
and some of the many
shapes of shells
to hunt for

The work of the waves never ceases.
Their power breaks rocks into boulders and
smooths boulders into pebbles and pebbles
into sand. Look around you for the interesting
shapes the sea has formed on your beach.

Every time a wave breaks...

...it wears away the shore and rocks

Sometimes where rocks have fallen
you can find fossils. Fossils were formed
thousands of years ago when the bodies
of sea creatures and plants were pressed
into mud and left impressions in the
rocks that formed around them.

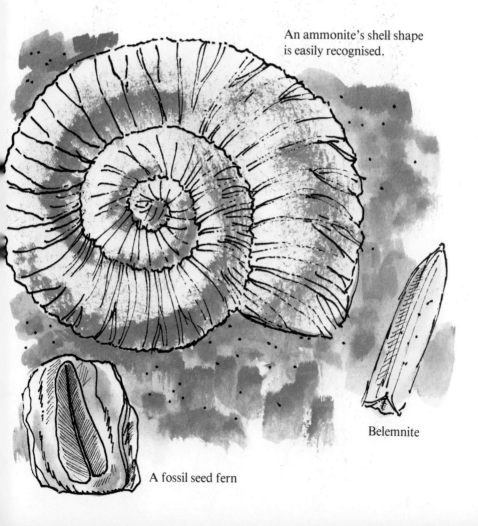

An ammonite's shell shape
is easily recognised.

Belemnite

A fossil seed fern

But while part of the coast is being lost
to the attacks of the sea, in some parts plants
are helping to create new ground.

Grasses, self-seeded or planted, like marron
and couch grass can put down long
rooting stems to bind the sand. There's a
grass that can survive even though covered
by the sea from time to time. Once these
grasses take hold and stop the sand from
shifting, other plants can start to grow and
form places for insects, birds and animals
to live…the land is really formed.

So this is the seashore. Always changing—
calm, stormy, windblown or baked in the sun,
there's a lot for you to find there.
Rocky or sandy, with pebbles or mud, what
kind of beach is the one you know?
And what can you find there?

First published 1979
Copyright © 1979 Denis Wrigley
ISBN 0 7188 2364 8
Printed in Hong Kong